Welcome to the PAPERBACK SONGS SERIES.

Do you play piano, guitar, electronic keyboard, sing or play any instrument for that matter? If so, this handy "pocket tune" book is for you.

The concise, one-line music notation consists of:

MELODY, LYRICS & CHORD SYMBOLS

Whether strumming the chords on guitar, "faking" an arrangement on piano/keyboard or singing the lyrics, these fake book style arrangements can be enjoyed at any experience level — hobbyist to professional.

The musical skills necessary to successfully use this book are minimal. If you play guitar and need some help with chords, a basic chord chart is included at the back of the book.

While playing and singing is the first thing that comes to mind when using this book, it can also serve as a compact, comprehensive reference guide.

However you choose to use this PAPERBACK SONGS SERIES book, by all means have fun!

CONTENTS

THE ROCK AND ROLL COLLECTION

MELODY LINE, CHORDS AND LYRICS FOR KEYBOARD • GUITAR • VOCAL

HAL•LEONARD

HAL•LEONARD™
CORPORATION
7777 W. BLUEMOUND RD. P.O. BOX 13819 MILWAUKEE, WI 53213

(contents continued)

AT THE HOP

**Words and Music by ARTHUR SINGER,
JOHN MADARA and DAVID WHITE**

Bright Rock

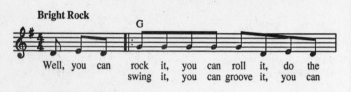

Well, you can rock it, you can roll it, do the
swing it, you can groove it, you can

stomp and e - ven stroll it At The Hop.
real - ly start to move it At The Hop.

When the rec - ord starts a spin - nin', you ca -
Where the jump - in' is the smooth - est and the

lyp - so when you chick - en At The Hop.
mu - sic is the cool - est At The Hop.

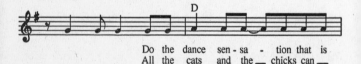

Do the dance sen - sa - tion that is
All the cats and the __ chicks can __

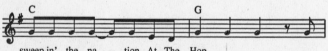

sweep - in' the na - tion At The Hop
get __ their kicks ____ At The Hop.

BABY, IT'S YOU

Words and Music by MACK DAVID,
BURT BACHARACH and BARNEY WILLIAMS

Moderately slow

It's not the way you smile_____ that touched my
You should hear what they say_____ a - bout_____

heart..
you.___
It's not the way you
They say you've nev - er

kiss that tears me a - part.___
nev - er nev - er been true.___

Man - y man - y
Does - n't mat - ter

nights roll by.__
what they say.__
I sit a - lone___ at
I know I'm gon - na love you

home and cry___ o - ver you.
any old way,___ what can I

What can I do?___ I can't help my -

self,___   'cause, Ba - by,   It's

You.___   Ba - by,   It's

You.___

do   when   it's   true?___

I   don't   want   no - bod - y,

'cause, Ba - by,   It's   You.___

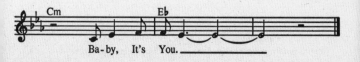

Ba - by,   It's   You. _____

BIRD DOG

Words and Music by
BOUDLEAUX BRYANT

Moderately

John-ny is a jok-er (He's a bird) A

ver-y fun-ny jok-er (He's a bird) But

when he jokes my hon-ey (He's a dog) His

jok-in' ain't so fun-ny (What a dog)

John-ny is the jok-er that's a-try-in' to steal my ba-by (He's a

Bird Dog)

13

THE BIRDS AND THE BEES

Words and Music by
HERB NEWMAN

Moderately, with a beat

G

Let me tell ya 'bout The Birds And The Bees and the

D7

flow - ers and the trees and the moon up a-bove

G

and a thing called love.

Let me tell ya 'bout the stars in the sky and a

D7

girl and a guy and the way they could kiss,

G

on a night like this.

G7   C

When I look in-to your big brown eyes

BITS AND PIECES

Words and Music by DAVE CLARK
and MIKE SMITH

I'm in piec - es, Bits And Piec - es.
I'm in piec - es, Bits And Piec - es.

Since you left me and you said good - bye. ___
You said you loved me and you'd al-ways be mine. ___

I'm in piec - es, Bits And Piec - es.
I'm in piec - es, Bits And Piec - es.

All I do is sit and cry. ___
We'd be to-geth-er till the end of time. ___

I'm in piec - es, Bits And Piec - es.
I'm in piec - es Bits And Piec - es.

You went a-way and left me mis - er - y. ___
Now you say it was just a game. ___

I'm in piec - es, Bits And Piec - es and
I'm in piec - es, Bits And Piec - es but

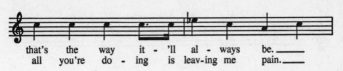

that's the way it - 'll al - ways be.
all you're do - ing is leav-ing me pain.

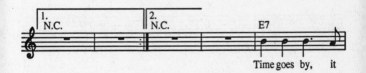

1.
N.C.
2.
N.C.
E7

Time goes by, it

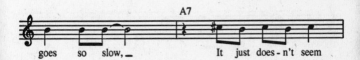

A7

goes so slow, It just does-n't seem

D7

true. On - ly just a

G7

few days a - go you said you loved me, nev - er

N.C. C F C

make me blue. I'm in piec - es,

F C F C

Bits And Piec - es. Now you're gone and I'm

all a - lone. ___ I'm in piec - es,

Bits And Piec - es. You're still way up there

on your own. ___ I'm in piec - es,

Bits And Piec - es. Noth - ing seems to

ev - er go right. ___ I'm in piec - es,

Bits And Piec - es. 'Cos night is day and

day is night. ___

ALL SHOOK UP

**Words and Music by OTIS BLACKWELL
and ELVIS PRESLEY**

Medium Shuffle Rhythm

A - well - a, bless my soul.__ What's
hands are sha - key and

wrong with me?__ I'm itch - ing like a man__ on a
my knees are weak I can't__ seem to stand__ on my

fuz - zy tree __ My friends say I'm act - in'
own two feet __ who do you thank when you

queer as a bug __ I'm in love
have __ such luck __ I'm in love I'm

All Shook Up! __ Mm __ mm oh, oh, yeah,

1. yeah! _____ My

21

BLUE SUEDE SHOES

Words and Music by
CARL LEE PERKINS

slan - der my name all o - ver the place;
drink _ my cider from my old - fruit jar;

Do an - y - thing that you want to do, _ but

uh - uh, hon - ey, lay off my shoes. _

Don't you step on my Blue Suede Shoes.

You can do an - y - thing _ but lay

off of my Blue Suede Shoes. _

Shoes. _

BLUEBERRY HILL

**Words and Music by AL LEWIS,
LARRY STOCK and VINCENT ROSE**

25

BO DIDDLEY

Words and Music by
ELLAS McDANIEL

Sun - day coat. ___
Sun - day hat. ___

Won't you come to my house and rack that bone, ___
Look at that ___ Bo - do oh where's he been, ___

Take my ba - by all the
Up to your house and

way from home.
gone a - gain.

Bo Did - dl - ey, Bo Did - dl - ey,

have you heard, ___ My.

___ pret - ty ba - by said she was a bird.

BOOK OF LOVE

Words and Music by WARREN DAVIS,
GEORGE MALONE and CHARLES PATRICK

Brightly

F   Dm   Gm7

Tell me, tell me, tell me, Oh, who wrote the Book Of

C7   F   Dm

Love? I've got to know the an-swer, Was it

Gm7   C7   F

some-one from a-bove? I won-der, won-der

Bb

who _____ who, Who wrote the Book Of

F

Love? _____ I _____ love you

Dm   Gm7

dar-ling ba-by you know I

C7   F   Dm

do but I've got to see this Book Of Love, _

BORN TO BE WILD

Words and Music by
MARS BONFIRE

Moderate Rock beat

Get your mo - tor run - ning.
I like smoke and light - ning,

Head out on the high - way
Heav - y me - tal thun - der

look - ing for ad - ven - ture in what
rac - ing in the wind and the

ev - er comes our way.
feel - ing that I'm un - der.

Yeah, dar - ling, gon - na make it hap - pen,

take the world in a love em - brace.

Fire all of your guns at once and

ex - plode _ in - to space. _____

Like a true _____ na - ture child _

we were born, ___ Born To Be Wild _

We have climbed _ so high, _____

nev - er want to die. _____

Born To Be Wild _____

Born To Be Wild, _____

Born To Be Wild,

Repeat and Fade

BUT IT'S ALRIGHT

Words and Music by JEROME L. JACKSON
and PIERRE TUBBS

33

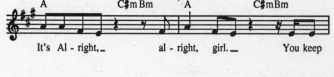

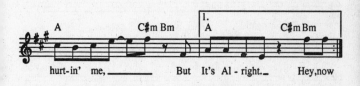

BREAKING UP
IS HARD TO DO

Words and Music by
HOWARD GREENFIELD and NEIL SEDAKA

BREATHLESS

Words and Music by OTIS BLACKWELL

BYE BYE, LOVE

Words and Music by
FELICE BRYANT and BOUDLEAUX BRYANT

CALENDAR GIRL

Words and Music by HOWARD GREENFIELD
and NEIL SADAKA

C

(March) I'm gon - na march you down the aisle,
ly) like a fire - crack - er I'm a - glow,

Am

(A - pril) you're the Eas - ter bun - ny when you smile.
(Au - gust) when you're on he beach you steal the show.

F   F#dim

Yeah, yeah, my heart's in a whirl. I

C/G   A7   3

love, I love, I love my lit - tle Cal - en - dar Girl ev - 'ry

D7   G7

day, ev - 'ry day of the

C   F6   1. C   2. C

year. (Sep -

tem - ber) I'll light the can - dles at your "sweet six - teen,"

CHANTILLY LACE

Words and Music by
J.P. RICHARDSON

Moderate Boogie Woogie

Chan - til - ly Lace and a pret - ty face and a pon - y tail hang - in' down, Wig - gle in her walk and a gig - gle in her talk, Makes the world go 'round, Ain't noth - in' in this world like a big-eyed girl to make me act so fun - ny, make me spend my mon - ey, make me feel real loose like a long-necked goose, like a girl.

CAN'T BUY ME LOVE

Words and Music by JOHN LENNON and PAUL McCARTNEY

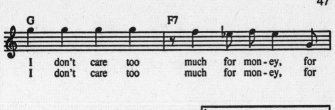

I don't care too much for mon-ey, for
I don't care too much for mon-ey, for

mon-ey can't buy me love. ___ I'll
mon-ey can't buy me love. _

___ { Can't Buy Me Love, ___

oh, ev-'ry-bod-y tells me so.__

___ Can't Buy Me Love, __ oh,

no no no__ no! Say you don't need no dia-

- mond rings__ and I'll be sat-is-fied,__

48

CHERISH

Words and Music by
TERRY KIRKMAN

(D.C.) Cher-ish is the word I use to de - scribe _____
Per - ish is the word that more than ap - plies _____

_____ all the feel-ing that I have hid-ing
to the hope in my heart each

here for you in - side. _____
time I re - a - lize _____

You don't know how man-y times I've wished that I had
that I am not gon-na be the one to share your

told you. You don't know how man-y times I've wished that I could
dreams. That I am not gon-na be the one to share your

hold you. You don't know how man-y times I've wished that I could
schemes. That I am not gon-na be the one to share what

mold you in - to some-one who could cher-ish me as much as
seems to be the life that you could cher-ish as much as

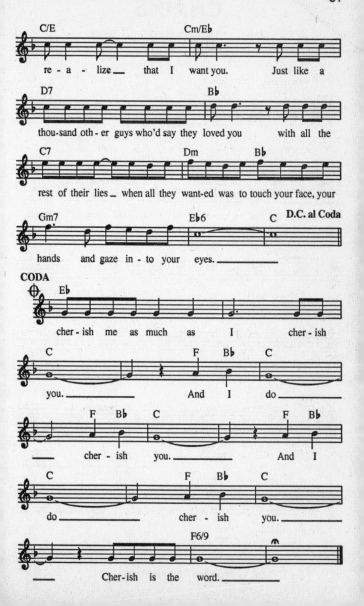

CHAINS

**Words and Music by GERRY GOFFIN
and CAROLE KING**

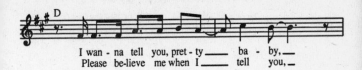

I wan - na tell you, pret - ty ____ ba - by, ___
Please be-lieve me when I ____ tell you, __

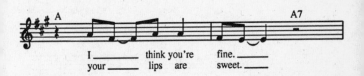

I ____ think you're fine. ____
your ____ lips are sweet. ____

I'd like to ____ love you, __ but
I'd like to ____ kiss them, __ but

D.C. (twice)
2nd time to Coda

dar - ling I'm im - pris - oned by ___ these
I can't break a - way .from all of these

CODA

Chains,

Repeat and Fade

Chains of love. _____

CHARLIE BROWN

Words and Music by JERRY LEIBER
and MIKE STOLLER

CRY LIKE A BABY

Words and Music by DAN PENN
snd SPOONER OLDHAM

Moderately bright

1., 3. When I think a-bout the good _ love you gave _ me, I
   2. *(See additional lyrics)*

Cry Like A Ba - by. _

Liv-ing with-out _ you is driv-ing me cra-zy; I

To Coda

Cry Like A Ba - by. _   *(Instrumental)*

Well, I know _ now, that you're not a play - thing;

not a toy, _ or a pup - et on a string. _

(Instrumental)

C/G G

2.

Am
To - day ___ we passed ___ on the street, ___

Em D C
and you just ___ walked on by; _____

Am
how my heart ___ just fell ___ to my feet, ___

Em D C7
and like a fool I be - gan to cry. _____

G
___ (Instrumental)

58

1. I know now that you're not a play - thing;
2. Ev - er - y road is a lone - ly street.
3., 4. etc. (See additional lyrics)

Cry Like A Ba - by, Cry Like A Ba - by.

Additional Lyrics

2. As I look back on a love so sweet,
   I Cry Like A Baby.
   Oh, every road is a lonely street;
   I Cry Like A Baby.
   I know that you're not a plaything;
   Not a toy, or a puppet on a string.

3. Living without you is driving me crazy;
   I Cry Like A Baby, Cry Like A Baby.

   Vocal ad lib. 4
   I cry, I cry, I cry,
   I cry, I Cry Like A Baby. *(etc.)*

DO YOU BELIEVE IN MAGIC

Words and Music by
JOHN SEBASTIAN

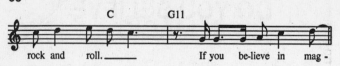

rock and roll.____ If you be-lieve in mag-

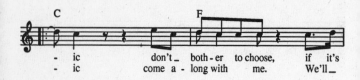

-ic don't _ both-er to choose, if it's
-ic come a - long with me. We'll _

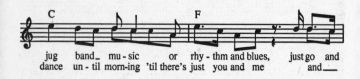

jug band _ mu - sic or rhy - thm and blues, just go and
dance un - til morn-ing 'til there's just you and me and_

lis - ten, it - 'll start with a smile that won't
may - be, if the mu - sic is right, I'll____

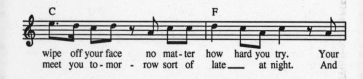

wipe off your face no mat - ter how hard you try. Your
meet you to - mor - row sort of late___ at night. And

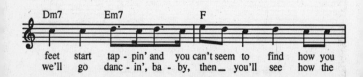

feet start tap - pin' and you can't seem to find how you
we'll go danc - in', ba - by, then_ you'll see how the

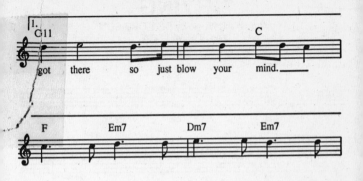

got there so just blow your mind.___

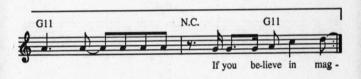

If you be-lieve in mag-

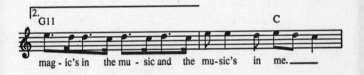

mag-ic's in the mu - sic and the mu-sic's in me.___

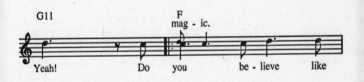

Yeah! Do you be - lieve like

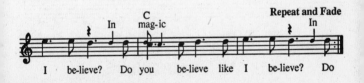

I be-lieve? Do you be-lieve like I be-lieve? Do

CRYING

**Words and Music by ROY ORBISON
and JOE MELSON**

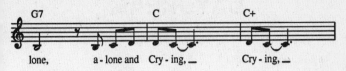

lone, a - lone and Cry - ing, __ Cry - ing, __

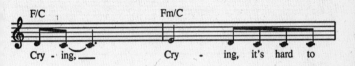

Cry - ing, __ Cry - ing, it's hard to

un - der - stand, but the touch of your

hand __ can start me Cry - ing. __

__ I thought that Cry - ing. __

Additional Lyrics

2. I thought that I was over you.
   But it's true, so true
   I love you even more than I did before.
   But darling, what can I do?
   For you don't love me and I'll always be
   Crying over you, Crying over you.
   Yes, now you're gone and from this moment on
   I'll be Crying, Crying, Crying, Crying
   Yeah, Crying, Crying over you.

DAYDREAM

Words and Music by
JOHN SEBASTIAN

What a day for a Day - dream, ___
I've been hav - ing a sweet - dream, ___
(Whistle)

What a day for a day - dream - in' boy. ___
I've been dream - in' since I woke up to - day. ___
(Whistle)

And I'm lost in a Day - dream, ___
It's star - ring me in my sweet ___ dream, ___
(Whistle)

Dream - in' 'bout my bun - dle of joy. ___
'Cause she's the one makes me feel ___ this way. ___
(Whistle) ___

And e - ven if time ain't real - ly
And e - ven if time is pass - ing me
And you can be sure that if you're

on my side, ___ It's one of those days for tak - ing a
by a lot, ___ I could - n't care less a - bout the
feel - in' right, ___ A Day - dream will last a - long ___

walk out - side. ____ I'm blow-ing the day to take a
dues you say I ____ got. To-mor-row I'll pay the dues for
in - to the night. ____ To-mor-row at break-fast you may

walk in the sun, ___ And fall on my face on some-bod-y's
drop-ping my load. _ A pie in the face for be - ing a
prick up your ears. ___

1.
new mowed lawn. _

2.
sleep - y bull toad. ___

CODA
Or you may be day-dream-in' for a thou-sand years. _

What a day for a Day - dream, _ Cus-tom made for a

day - dream - in' boy. ___ And I'm lost in a Day -

- dream, ___ Dream-in' 'bout my bun-dle of joy. _

(Whistle) ____

Repeat and Fade

(Whistle) ____

DON'T SAY NOTHIN' BAD
(ABOUT MY BABY)
Words and Music by GERRY GOFFIN and CAROLE KING

Additional Lyrics

2. Don't you tell me my baby's just a playboy (It isn't true).
   Don't you tell me my baby's just a playboy (That's a lie).
   I won't listen to a single word you say, boy (He's my guy).
   Don't you tell me my baby's just a playboy.
   (He's true) He's true (He's true to me), true to me.
   (So girl, you better shut your mouth.)*(To Bridge)*

3. *Repeat 1st Verse (To Coda)*

DREAM BABY
(HOW LONG MUST I DREAM)

Words and Music by
CINDY WALKER

Moderately

Dream Ba - by got___ me dream-in' sweet dreams

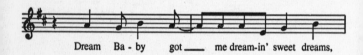

the whole day through.

Dream Ba - by got___ me dream-in' sweet dreams,

night time too.

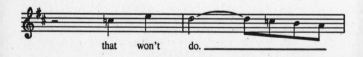

I love you and___ I'm dream-in' of you,

that won't do. ___

DUKE OF EARL

**Words and Music by EARL EDWARDS,
EUGENE DIXON and BERNICE WILLIAMS**

DON'T BE CRUEL
(To A Heart That's True)

Words and Music by OTIS BLACKWELL
and ELVIS PRESLEY

72

73

THE END OF THE WORLD

Words by SYLVIA DEE
Music by ARTHUR KENT

Slowly

Why does the sun go on shin-ing?

Why does the sea rush to shore? Don't they know it's The

End Of The World, 'Cause you don't love me an-y-

more? Why do the birds go on

sing-ing? Why do the stars glow a-

bove? Don't they know it's The

End Of The World? It end-ed when I lost your

FROM ME TO YOU

**Words and Music by JOHN LENNON
and PAUL McCARTNEY**

Moderately

Da da da   da da dum dum da._____ Da da

da   da da dum dum   da._____ If there's

an-y-thing that you   want,_____ if there's
ev-'ry-thing that you   want,_____ Like a

an-y-thing I can do._____ } Just
heart__ that's   oh so   true,_____

call on   me__ and I'll send it a-long__ with love.

__ From Me__ To You._____ I've got

1. C

__ I've got arms   that long to

2. C   Gm7

78

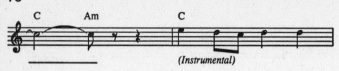

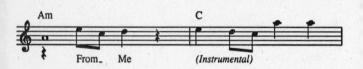

From Me (Instrumental)

To You. Just call on me and I'll

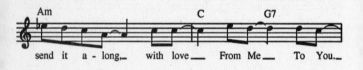

send it a-long, with love From Me To You.

I've got To you, to you,

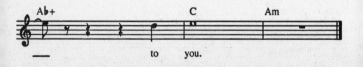

to you.

GOOD LOVIN'

Words and Music by
RUDY CLARK and ART RESNICK

— to have love. Good Lov - in', { ev - 'ry - bod - y / hey now you } got —

— to have love. Good Lov - in' lit - tle bit of love._

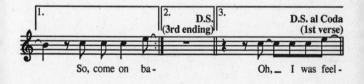

Now ba - by good love.

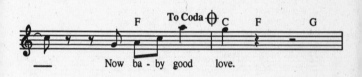

(Instrumental)

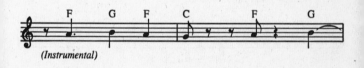

So, come on ba - Oh, _ I was feel-

Lov - in'. Say a - gain _ now, Good

GIMME SOME LOVIN'

Words and Music by SPENCER DAVIS,
MUFF WINWOOD and STEVE WINWOOD

GOIN' OUT OF MY HEAD

Words and Music by TEDDY RANDAZZO
and BOBBY WEINSTEIN

GOOD LUCK CHARM

Words and Music by AARON SCHROEDER
and WALLY GOLD

Moderately

Don't want a four leaf clov - er;
Don't want a sil - ver dol - lar,
I found a luck - y pen - ny, I'd

don't want an old horse shoe.
rab - bit's foot __ on a string. The
toss it a - cross the bay. Your

Want your kiss __ 'cause I just can't miss __ with a
hap - pi - ness __ in your warm ca - ress __ no __
love is worth __ all the gold on earth; __ no __

Good Luck Charm like you.
rab - bit's foot can bring. } Come on and
won - der that I say:

be my lit - tle Good Luck Charm. __ Uh-huh - huh,

__ you sweet de - light. __ I want a

Good Luck Charm __ a - hang - in' on my arm __ To have, __

GOOD ROCKIN' TONIGHT

By ROY BROWN

In genuine rockabilly

Well, I heard the news: there's Good Rock-in' To-night.
heard the news? Ev- 'ry-bod-y's rock-in' to-night.

Well, I heard the news: there's
Have you heard the news? Ev -

a Good Rock-in' To-night. }
-'ry-bod-y's rock-in' to-night. }
I wan-na

hold my baby tight as I can; to-

night she'll know I'm a might-y, might-y man. I

heard the news: there's Good Rock-in' To-night.

I say he'll meet me in a hur-ry, be-hind the barn. Don't

you be a-fraid, dar-lin', I'll do you no harm._ I

want you to bring_ a-long my rock-in' shoes_ 'cause to-

night I'm gon-na rock a-way all the blues. I heard the news:_

there's Good Rock-in' To-night._ *(Instrumental)*

Well,_ we gon-na

rock. We gon-na rock.

A7

Let's rock, come on and

E B7

rock. We gon-na rock all

E D.S. al Coda

our blues a - way. Have you

CODA

Well, we're gon-na rock, rock,

rock. Ah, come on and rock, rock,

A7

rock, al-ways rock, rock, rock. Ah, well, let's

E B

rock, rock, rock. Ah, we gon-na rock all

E7 E6

our blues a - way.

GREAT BALLS OF FIRE

**Words and Music by OTIS BLACKWELL
and JACK HAMMER**

Bright Rock

You shake my nerves and you *(Instrumental)* rat-tle my brain. Too much love drives a man in-sane. You broke my will, but what a thrill. Good-ness gra-cious, Great Balls Of Fire! I laughed at love 'cause I thought it was fun-ny. You came a-long and you moved.

me, hon - ey.   I changed my mind,

love's just fine. __   Good - ness gra - cious, Great __

__ Balls Of Fire!
Instrumental ends   Kiss me, ba - by.

Woo, _____

__ it feels good.   Hold me, ba - by.

Girl, just let me love you like a
I want to love you like a

lov - er should. __
lov - er should. __   You're fine, __

so kind, ___ I'm gon-na tell the world that you're

mine, mine, mine, mine. ___ I chew my nails and I

twid-dle my thumb. ___ I'm real ner-vous but it

sure is fun. ___ Come on, ba - by, you're

driv-ing me cra - zy. Good - ness gra - cious, Great

___ Balls Of Fire! Good - ness gra - cious, Great

___ Balls Of Fire!

THE GREEN DOOR

Words and Music by BOB DAVIE
and MARVIN MOORE

old pi - a - no and they play it hot __ be-hind The
eye - ball peep - in' thru a smok - y cloud. __ be-hind The

Green Door. __ Don't know
Green Door. __ When I

what they're do - in' but they laugh a lot __ be-hind The
said Joe sent __ me some-one laughed out loud __ be-hind The

Green Door. __ Wish they'd
Green Door. __ All I

let me in __ so I could find out what's __ be-hind The
want to do __ is join the hap - py crew __ be-hind The

1.
Green Door. ___

2.
Green Door. ___

A GROOVY KIND OF LOVE

Words and Music by TONI WINE
and CAROLE BAYER SAGER

Moderately slow

When I'm feel-in' blue, all I have to
want to you can turn me

do is take a look at you, then I'm not so
on to an-y-thing you want to, an-y-time at

blue. When you're close to me I can feel your
all. When I taste your lips, oh, I start to

heart beat I can hear you breath-ing in my
shiv-er can't con-trol the quiv-er-ing in-

ear. } Would-n't you a-gree, ba-by you and
side.

me got a groov-y kind of love?

We got a groov-y kind of love.

97

HANKY PANKY

Words and Music by JEFF BARRY
and ELLIE GREENWICH

Moderate Boogie–Rock

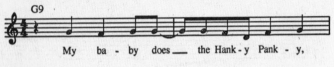

My ba - by does __ the Hank - y Pank - y,

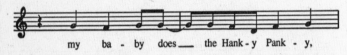

my ba - by does __ the Hank - y Pank - y,

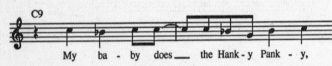

My ba - by does __ the Hank - y Pank - y,

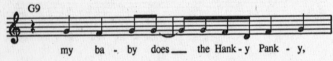

my ba - by does __ the Hank - y Pank - y,

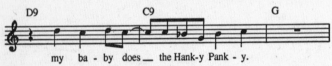

my ba - by does __ the Hank - y Pank - y.

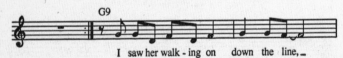

I saw her walk - ing on down the line, __

You know I saw her for the ver - y first time, __

HAPPY TOGETHER

Words and Music by GARRY BONNER
and ALAN GORDON

baby, the skies will be blue for all my life.

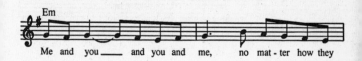

Me and you and you and me, no mat - ter how they

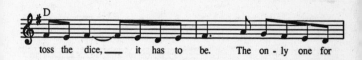

toss the dice, it has to be. The on - ly one for

To Coda

me is you, and you for me, so Hap - py To -

D.S. al Coda (with repeat)

geth - er. Im - ag - ine

CODA

geth - er. / weath - er? So Hap - py To -

Repeat and Fade

geth - er. How is the

HAPPY, HAPPY BIRTHDAY BABY

Words and Music by MARGO SYLVIA
and GILBERT LOPEZ

Hap - py, Hap - py Birth - day, Ba - by. ___

Although you're ___ with some - bod - y new; ___

Thought I'd drop a line to say that I wish this ___ hap-py

day would find me ___ be - side you. ___

___ Hap - py, Hap - py Birth - day, Ba - by. ___

No, I can't call you my ba - by; ___

Seems like years a - go we met on a day I ___ can't for-

ARD DAY'S NIGHT

ords and Music by JOHN LENNON
and PAUL McCARTNEY

ev - 'ry - thing seems __ to be al -

right. When I'm home. __

feel - ing you hold - ing me tight,

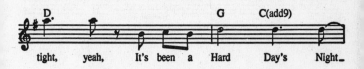

tight, yeah, It's been a Hard Day's Night __

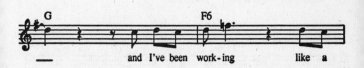

__ and I've been work - ing like a

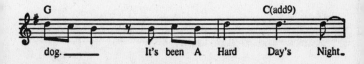

dog. __ It's been A Hard Day's Night __

I should be sleep-ing like a log._ But when I get home to you_ I find the thing that you do_ will make me feel_ al - right.._

(Instrumental)

So why I

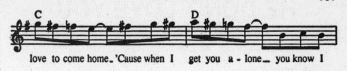

love to come home. 'Cause when I get you a - lone_ you know I

feel_ O. _ K. _ When I'm home_

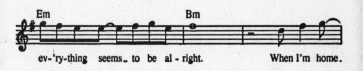

ev-'ry-thing seems_ to be al - right. When I'm home.

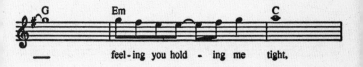

_ feel-ing you hold - ing me tight,

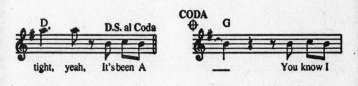

tight, yeah, It's been A _ You know I

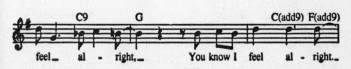

feel_ al - right,_ You know I feel al - right._

(Instrumental)

HE DON'T LOVE YOU
(LIKE I LOVE YOU)
Words and Music by JERRY BUTLER, CALVIN CARTER and CURTIS MAYFIELD

Moderately

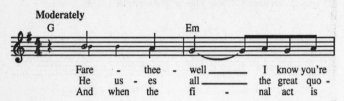

Fare - thee - well _____ I know you're
He us - es all _____ the great quo-
And when the fi - nal act is

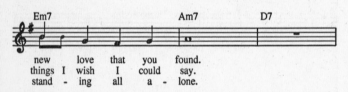

leav - ing, For the
ta - tions, He says
o - ver, And you're left

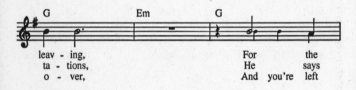

new love that you found.
things I wish I could say.
stand - ing all a - lone.

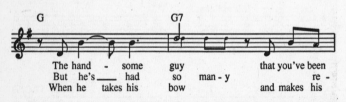

The hand - some guy that you've been
But he's ___ had so man - y re-
When he takes his bow and makes his

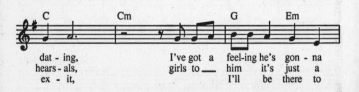

dat - ing, I've got a feel-ing he's gon - na
hears - als, girls to him it's just a
ex - it, I'll be there to

HEARTBREAK HOTEL

Words and Music by MAE BOREN AXTON,
TOMMY DURDEN and ELVIS PRESLEY

Moderate Blues

1. Now, since my ba-by left me I've found a
2.,3. *(See additional lyrics)*

new place to dwell, down at the end __ of Lone-ly Street at

Heart - break Ho-tel. I'm so

lone - ly, _____ I'm so lone - ly, _____ I'm so

lone - ly, _____ that I could die; and

tho' it's al - ways crowd-ed, you __ can still find some room

for bro - ken - heart - ed lov - ers to

cry there in ___ the gloom and be so

lone - ly, ___ oh, so lone - ly, ___ oh, so

lone - ly ___ they could die.

2. The die.
3. So,

Additional Lyrics

2. The bellhop's tears keep flowing,
   The desk clerk's dressed in black...
   They've been so long on Lonely Street,
   They never will go back.
   And they're so lonely
   Oh, they're so lonely.
   They're so lonely
   They pray to die.

3. So, if your baby leaves
   And you have a tale to tell,
   Just take a walk down Lonely Street
   To Heartbreak Hotel,
   Where you'll be so lonely
   And I'll be so lonely.
   We'll be so lonely
   That we could die.

HELLO MARY LOU

Words and Music by GENE PITNEY
and C. MANGIARACINA

Moderately

You passed me by one sun-ny day ___ and, flashed those big brown eyes my way and, oo, I want-ed you for-ev-er-more. ___ Now I'm not one that gets a-round, ___ I swear my feet stuck to the ground, and though I nev-er did meet you be-fore. ___

saw your lips I heard your voice, ___ be-lieve me I just had no choice, wild hors-es could-n't make me stay a-way. ___ I thought a-bout a moon-lit night, ___ my arms a-bout you good an' tight, that's all I had to see for me to say. ___

HIPPY HIPPY SHAKE

Words and Music by
CHAN ROMERO

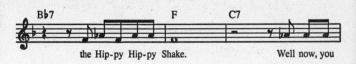

the Hip-py Hip-py Shake. Well now, you

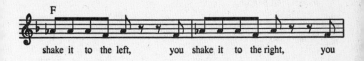

shake it to the left, you shake it to the right, you

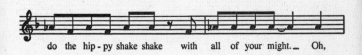

do the hip-py shake shake with all of your might.__ Oh,

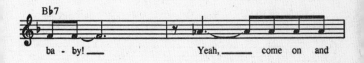

ba - by! __ Yeah, _____ come on and

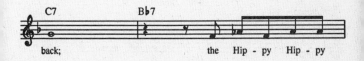

shake. Yeah, _____ it's in the

back; the Hip - py Hip - py

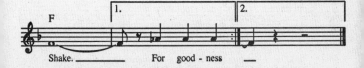

Shake. _____ For good - ness __

HIS LATEST FLAME

Words and Music by
DOC POMUS and MORT SHUMAN

Moderately bright

A ver-y old friend came by to-
talked, and I heard him

day. 'Cause he was tell - in' ev - 'ry -
say that she had the long - est

one in town_ 'bout the love that he just found._
black - est hair,_ the pret - tiest green eyes an - y - where._

And Ma-rie's the name of His Lat - est
And Ma-rie's the name of His Lat - est

Flame. He talked and
Flame.

Though I smiled, the tears in - side_ were a - burn-in'._

I wished him luck and then he said_ good-

HOUND DOG

**Words and Music by JERRY LEIBER
and MIKE STOLLER**

Medium Bright Rock

You ain't noth-in' but a Hound Dog, ___ cry-in' all the time.

You ain't noth-in' but a Hound Dog, ___ cry-in' all the time.

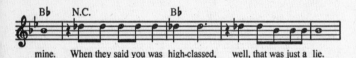

Well, ___ you ain't nev-er caught a rab-bit and you ain't no friend ___ of

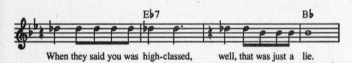

mine. When they said you was high-classed, well, that was just a lie.

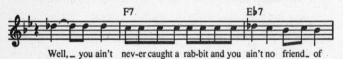

When they said you was high-classed, well, that was just a lie.

Well, ___ you ain't nev-er caught a rab-bit and you ain't no friend ___ of

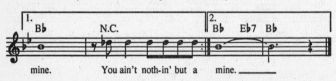

mine. You ain't noth-in' but a | mine. ___

I SAW HER STANDING THERE

Words and Music by JOHN LENNON
and PAUL McCARTNEY

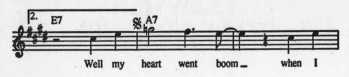

Well my heart went boom___ when I

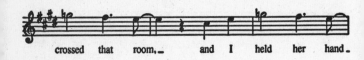

crossed that room,___ and I held her hand___

___ in mi - een, ___ een, ___

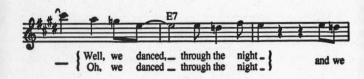

___ { Well, we danced,___ through the night ___ } and we
     { Oh, we danced ___ through the night ___ }

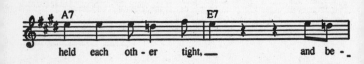

held each oth - er tight, ___ and be -.

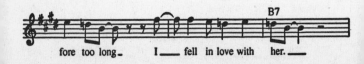

fore too long ___ I ___ fell in love with her. ___

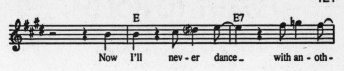

Now I'll nev - er dance _ with an - oth -

- er, _ Oh, _ since I Saw Her

Stand - ing There. _ Well my

CODA

_ Oh, since I Saw _

_ Her Stand - ing There. _

Yeah, well since I Saw _ Her Stand - ing There. _

_ (Instrumental)

I WANT TO HOLD YOUR HAND

**Words and Music by JOHN LENNON
and PAUL McCARTNEY**

Moderately

G   D

Oh yeah, I'll _____ tell you some - thing
please _____ say to me _____

Em   Bm   G

I think you'll un - der - stand. When I _____ say that
you'll let me be your man, And please _____ say to

D   Em   Bm

some - thing, I Want To Hold Your Hand, ___
me _____ you'll let me hold your hand, ___

C   D   G   Em

I Want To Hold Your Hand, _____
Now let me hold your hand, _____

C   D   1. G   2. G

I Want To Hold Your Hand. Oh, ___
I Want To Hold Your Hand.

Dm7   G

And when I touch you I feel

C   Am   Dm7

hap - py _____ in - side. _____ It's such a

LEADER OF THE PACK

Words and Music by GEORGE MORTON,
JEFF BARRY and ELLIE GREENWICH

Moderately, with a beat

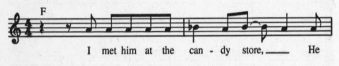

I met him at the can - dy store, ___ He

turned a - round and smiled at me, you get the pic - ture? *Yes, we see.*

That's when I fell for the Lead - er Of The

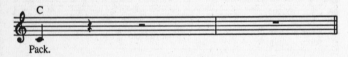

Pack.

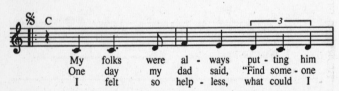

My folks were al - ways put - ting him
One day my dad said, "Find some - one
I felt so help - less, what could I

down. ___
new." ___
do? ___

They said he came from the wrong side of
I had to tell my ___ Jim - my we're
Re - mem - b'ring all the ___ things we'd been

Bb **G** **To Coda**

town. ___
through. ___
through. ___

F

They told me he was bad, ___
He stood there and asked me why, ___

Em

But I know he was sad, ___
But all I could do was cry, ___

G7

That's why I fell for the Lead - er Of The
I'm sor - ry I hurt you, the Lead - er Of The

1.
C

Pack.

2.
C **Bm**

Pack.

126

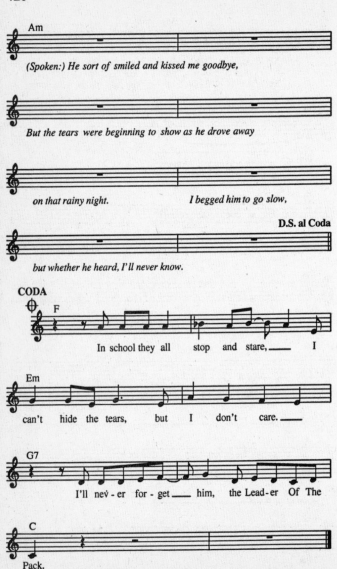

Am

(Spoken:) He sort of smiled and kissed me goodbye,

But the tears were beginning to show as he drove away

on that rainy night.   *I begged him to go slow,*

D.S. al Coda

but whether he heard, I'll never know.

CODA

F

In school they all stop and stare, ___ I

Em

can't hide the tears, but I don't care. ___

G7

I'll nev̇-er for-get ___ him, the Lead-er Of The

C

Pack.

I WILL FOLLOW HIM

(a/k/a I WILL FOLLOW YOU)

English Lyric by NORMAN GIMBEL and ARTHUR ALTMAN
Original Lyric by JACQUES PLANTE
Music by J.W. STOLE and DEL ROMA

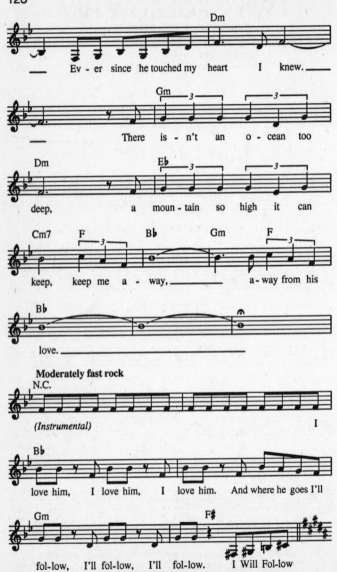

Ev - er since he touched my heart I knew.

There is - n't an o - cean too

deep, a moun - tain so high it can

keep, keep me a - way, a - way from his

love.

Moderately fast rock

N.C.

(Instrumental)

love him, I love him, I love him. And where he goes I'll

fol-low, I'll fol-low, I'll fol-low. I Will Fol-low

is - n't an o - cean too deep, a

moun - tain so high it can keep, keep us a -

way, a - way from his love.

(I love him,) oh, yes, I

love ____ him. (I'll fol - low,) I'm gon - na

fol - low. ____ (True love,) he'll al - ways be my

true ____ love. (For - ev - er,) from now un - til for -

I'M INTO SOMETHING GOOD

Words and Music by GERRY GOFFIN and CAROLE KING

Moderately, with a beat

Woke up this morn - in' ___ feel - in' fine, ___ I
When he walked me home and he held my hand, ___ I

felt like the world was my Val - en - time. ___
knew it would-n't be just a one night stand ___ 'cause

Last night I met a new boy in the neigh - bor -
he asked to see me next week and I told him he

hood, ___ and some-thing tells me
could. ___ Some-thing tells me

I'm In - to Some - thing Good. ___
I'm In - to Some - thing

Good. ___

He's kind of qui - et but not too shy, ___

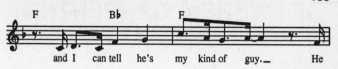

and I can tell he's my kind of guy._ He

danced ev - 'ry slow dance with me like I hoped he would._

Some-thing tells me I'm In - to Some-thing

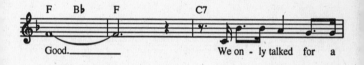

Good._ We on - ly talked for a

min - ute or two_ and I felt like I knew him_ my

whole life through. _ I don't know if you can call it love,_ but

D.C. al Fine

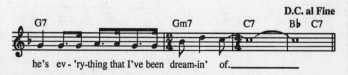

he's ev - 'ry-thing that I've been dream-in' of._

IF I WERE A CARPENTER

Words and Music by
TIM HARDIN

Moderately

If I___ Were A Car-pen-ter___
If I___ worked my hands in wood,_

and you were a la-dy,
would you still love me?

would you mar-ry me an-y-way?
An-swer me, babe, "Yes, I would,

Would you have my ba-by?
I'd put you a-bove me."

If a tink-er
If I were a

were my trade,_
mil-ler,

would you still
at a mill-wheel

love me?
grind-ing,

Car-ry-ing the
would you miss your

135

IN THE STILL OF THE NITE

(I'LL REMEMBER)

Words and Music by
FRED PARRIS

IT'S MY PARTY

Words and Music by HERB WIENER, WALLY GOLD and JOHN GLUCK, JR.

Moderately bright

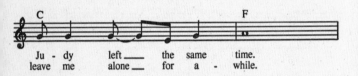

1. No - bod - y knows where my John - ny has gone, but
2. Play all my rec - ords, keep danc - ing all night, but
3. *(See additional lyrics)*

Ju - dy left the same time.
leave me alone for a - while.

Why was he hold - ing her hand, when
'Til John - ny's danc - ing with me, I've

he's sup - posed to be mine?
got no rea - son to smile.

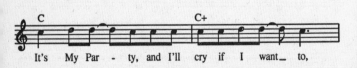

It's My Par - ty, and I'll cry if I want to,

F
Fm
cry if I want_ to, cry if I want_ to,
C
G7
C
F
C
you would cry, too, if it hap-pened to you.
1.
G7
2.
C

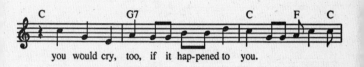

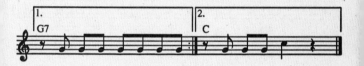

Additional Lyrics

3. Judy and Johnny just walked thru the door,
   Like a queen with her king,
   Oh, what a birthday surprise,
   Judy's wearing his ring.

JUST ONE LOOK

Words and Music by
DORIS PAYNE and GREGORY CARROLL

and al - ways.___ Oh,___ oh,___

Just One Look.___ and I knew - ew ew.___

___ that___ you___ were my on - ly___

one.___ Oh_____ I thought I was

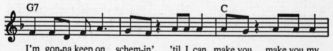

dream-in', but I was wrong.___ Oh yeah,___ yeah,___ ah, but

I'm gon-na keep on schem-in' 'til I can make you, make you my

own.___   Just One Look,.   that's all it took { yeah. } { wow. }

LITTLE DARLIN'

Words and Music by
MAURICE WILLIAMS

just
for — you,

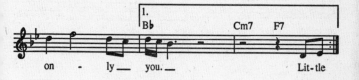

on - ly — you. —
Lit-tle

you. _____

Additional Lyrics
(May be spoken over repeat of Chorus)

2. My dear, I need your love to call my own
   And never do wrong; and to hold in mine your little hand.
   I'll know too soon that I'll love again.
   Please come back to me.

LONG TALL SALLY

Words and Music by ENOTRIS JOHNSON,
RICHARD PENNIMAN and ROBERT BLACKWELL

Bright Rock tempo

Gon - na tell Aunt Ma - - ry
Long Tall Sal - ly has a
saw Un - cle John with

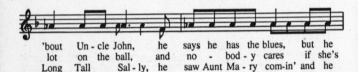

'bout Un - cle John, he says he has the blues, but he
lot on the ball, and no - bod - y cares if she's
Long Tall Sal - ly, he saw Aunt Ma - ry com - in' and he

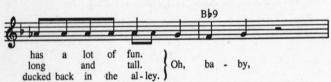

has a lot of fun.
long and tall. } Oh, ba - by,
ducked back in the al - ley. }

yes _____ ba - by

woo _____ ba - by, _____

Hav - in' me some fun to - night. _____

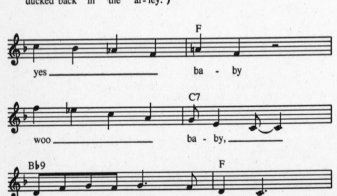

LOVE ME DO

Words and Music by JOHN LENNON and PAUL McCARTNEY

MY BOYFRIEND'S BACK

Words and Music by ROBERT FELDMAN, GERALD GOLDSTEIN and RICHARD GOTTEHRER

Moderately

My Boy-friend's Back, and you're gon-na be in trou-ble.
He's been gone for such a long time. ___

(Hey, la - di - la, My Boy-friend's Back)

When you

see him com-in' bet-ter cut on the dou-ble.
Now he's back and things will be fine. ___

(Hey, la - di - la, My Boy-friend's Back)

You're

You've been spread-in' lies that I was un-true. ___
gon-na be sor-ry you ev-er were born. ___

(Hey, la - di - la, My Boy-friend's Back)

So

'Cause he's

look out now 'cause he's com-in' af-ter you. ___
kind of big and he's aw-ful strong. ___

(Hey, la - di - la, My Boy-friend's Back)

And ____ he knows that you've been try - in',
And ____ he knows a - bout your cheat-in',

and ____ he knows that you've been ly - in',
now ____ you're gon - na get a beat-in',

What made you think he'd be - lieve all your lies? ____ (Ah -

oo ____ Ah - oo) You're a

big man now but he'll cut you down to size! ____ (Ah -

oo) Wait and see! ____ My

Boy - friend's Back, He's gon - na save my rep - u - ta - tion.

(Hey, la - di - la, My Boy-friend's Back)

If

I were you I'd take a per - ma - nent va - ca - tion.

(Hey, la - di - la, My Boy-friend's Back)

La - di - la, My Boy-friend's Back!

Repeat and Fade

La - di - la, My Boy-friend's Back!

MAYBE BABY

By NORMAN PETTY
and CHARLES HARDIN

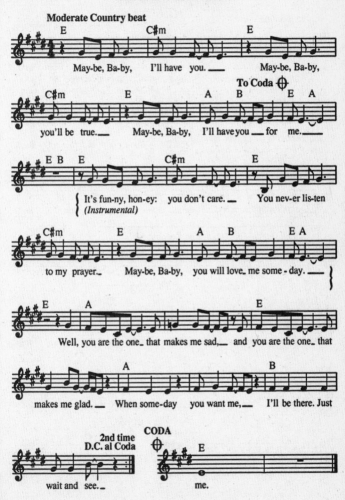

May-be, Ba-by, I'll have you. ___ May-be, Baby, you'll be true. ___ May-be, Ba-by, I'll have you ___ for me.

It's fun-ny, hon-ey: you don't care. ___ You nev-er lis-ten
(Instrumental)

to my prayer. ___ May-be, Ba-by, you will love me some - day. ___

Well, you are the one ___ that makes me sad, ___ and you are the one ___ that makes me glad. ___ When some-day you want me, ___ I'll be there. Just

2nd time
D.C. al Coda

CODA

wait and see. ___ me.

OH BOY!

Words and Music by SUNNY WEST,
BILL TILGHMAN and NORMAN PETTY

ON BROADWAY

Words and Music by BARRY MANN,
CYNTHIA WEIL, MIKE STOLLER and JERRY LEIBER

They say the ne-on lights are bright.
They say the wom-en treat you fine On Broadway;
They say that I won't last too long

They say there's al-ways mag-ic in the air;
But look-in' at them just gives me the blues;
I'll catch a Grey-hound bus for home, they say;

But when you're walk-in'
'Cause how ya gon-na
But they're dead wrong, I

down the street, And you ain't had e-nough to eat,
make some time, When all you got is one thin dime,
know they are. 'Cause I can play this here gui-tar,

1.,2.
The glit-ter rubs right off and you're no-where.
And one thin dime won't e-ven shine your shoes.
And I won't quit till

3.
I'm a star. On Broad-way.

OH, PRETTY WOMAN

Words and Music by ROY ORBISON
and BILL DEES

1. Pret-ty Wom-an, __ walk-ing down the street; __ Pret-ty
2. *(See additional lyrics)*

Wom-an, __ the kind I like to meet, __ Pret-ty

Wom-an, __ I don't be - lieve you; __ you're not the

truth. __ No one could look as good as you. __

__ *Spoken: Mer - cy.* __ *(Instrumental)*

1.

2. Pret - ty

2.

Pret-ty Wom - an, stop a - while, __

156

Dm · · · Bbm · · · C7 · · ·
ba - by, _____ be mine to - night. _____

Pret - ty

F · · · Dm · · ·
Wom - an, ___ don't walk on by; ___ Pret - ty

F · · · Dm · · ·
Wom - an, ___ don't make me cry; ___ Pret - ty

Bb · · · C7 · · ·
Wom - an, _____ don't walk a - way. _

Hey, _____ O. K. _____

_ If that's the way it must be, O.

K. _____ I guess I'll go on home; _ it's

Additional Lyrics

2. Pretty Woman, won't you pardon me?
   Pretty Woman, I couldn't help but see;
   Pretty Woman, that you look lovely as can be.
   Are you lonely just like me?

ONE FINE DAY

Words and Music by GERRY GOFFIN
and CAROLE KING

Briskly

One___ fine day ___
The arms I long for ___
One___ fine day ___

you'll look at me, ___
will o-pen wide, ___
we'll meet once more, ___

and you will know___ our love was
and you'll be proud___ to have me
and then you'll want___ the love you

meant___ to be.
walk-ing by your side. ___
threw a-way be-fore. ___

One___ Fine Day___

you're gon-na want me for your

girl. *(Instrumental)*

G   **F/G**   **G**   **C**   **Bb/C**

dar - ling, _   you'll come to me when you _

D.C. al Coda   **CODA**

Gm7/C   **Bb/C**   **C**   **F**

want to set-tle down, oh.   girl. One _ Fine

Dm11   **Dm7**   **Bb**   **C**

Day,_____   oh,   oh, _____

F   **Dm11**   **Dm7**   **Bb**

_   One _ Fine Day_____   you're gon-na

C   **F**   **Dm7**

want me for your   girl.   Shoo-be-do-be-do-be - do-be-do wah,   wah,
(Lead vocal 1st time only)

Bb   **Gm7/C**   **F**

shoo-be-do-be-do-be - do-be-do wah,   wah.   *(Instrumental)*

Dm7   **Bb**   **Bb/C**   **Repeat and Fade**

PIPELINE

Words and Music by BOB SPICKARD
and BRIAN CARMAN

ONLY THE LONELY
(KNOW THE WAY I FEEL)

Words and Music by ROY ORBISON
and JOE MELSON

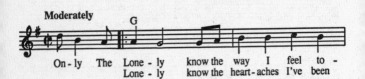

On - ly The Lone - ly know the way I feel to -
Lone - ly know the heart - aches I've been

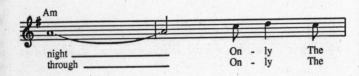

night _____ On - ly The
through _____ On - ly The

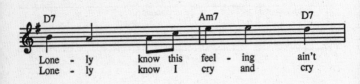

Lone - ly know this feel - ing ain't
Lone - ly know I cry and cry

right _____ you There goes my ba - by _____
for you May - be to - mor - row,

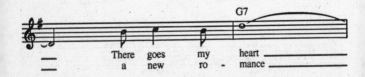

There goes my heart _____
a new ro - mance

PEGGY SUE

Words and Music by JERRY ALLISON,
NORMAN PETTY and BUDDY HOLLY

Brightly

If you knew __ Peg - gy Sue,
Peg - gy Sue, __ Peg - gy Sue, __

__ Then you'd
Oh, how

know why I feel blue __
my heart yearns for you, __

__ A - bout Peg - gy,
Oh, Pa - heg - gy,

__ 'Bout my Peg - gy Sue;
My Pa - heg - gy Sue;

Oh, well, I love you, gal, __ Yes, I

love you, Peg - gy Sue:___

Peg - gy Sue,___ Peg - gy Sue,___

___ Pret - ty, pret - ty, pret - ty, pret - ty,

Peg - gy Sue,___ Oh, my Peg - gy, ___

___ My Peg - gy Sue; ___

Oh, well, I love you gal, ___ and I

need you, Peg - gy Sue.___

REBEL-'ROUSER

**Words and Music by DUANE EDDY
and LEE HAZLEWOOD**

PLEASE PLEASE ME

**Words and Music by JOHN LENNON
and PAUL McCARTNEY**

169

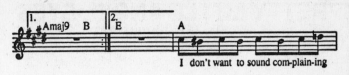

I don't want to sound com-plain-ing

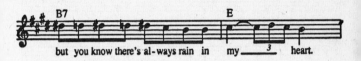

but you know there's al-ways rain in my___ ³ heart.

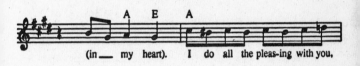

(in___ my heart). I do all the pleas-ing with you,

it's so hard to rea-son with you, wo

D.C. al Coda

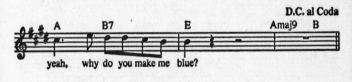

yeah, why do you make me blue?

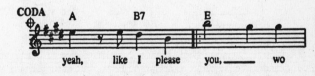

CODA

yeah, like I please you,___ wo

yeah, like I please you.___

PRETTY LITTLE ANGEL EYES

Words and Music by TOMMY BOYCE
and CURTIS LEE

let you go___ be-cause_ I love_ you my dar-ling
heav-en - ly___ you know_ I love_ you my dar-ling

an - gel eyes.___ Pret-ty lit-tle, lit-tle, lit-tle
an - gel

an - gel eyes.___ eyes. (Oh an - gel eyes.___)

I know you were sent from heav-en a-

bove ___ to fill my life with your won-der-ful

love, ___ know we'll be hap-py for e - ter-ni-ty,___

___ 'cause there's no-o-o-o-no-where that I'd rath-er be.

D.S. al Coda

CODA

an - gel

eyes.
(Oh an - gel eyes. ___)

RETURN TO SENDER

Words and Music by
OTIS BLACKWELL and WINFIELD SCOTT

ROCK AROUND THE CLOCK

By MAX C. FREEDMAN
and JIMMY DeKNIGHT

rock,   rock,   rock,   'til   broad day - light, — We're gon - na

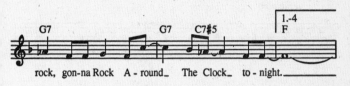

rock, gon-na Rock A - round— The Clock— to - night.

—   When the

Additional Lyrics

2. When the clock strikes two, and three and four,
   If the band slows down we'll yell for more,
   We're gonna Rock Around The Clock tonight,
   We're gonna rock, rock, rock 'til broad daylight,
   We're gonna rock, gonna Rock Around The Clock tonight.

3. When the clock chimes ring five and six and seven,
   We'll be rockin' up in seventh heav'n,
   We're gonna Rock Around The Clock tonight,
   We're gonna rock, rock, rock 'til broad daylight,
   We're gonna rock, gonna Rock Around The Clock tonight.

4. When it's eight, nine, ten, eleven, too,
   I'll be goin' strong and so will you,
   We're gonna Rock Around The Clock tonight,
   We're gonna rock, rock, rock 'til broad daylight,
   We're gonna rock, gonna Rock Around The Clock tonight.

5. When the clock strikes twelve, we'll cool off, then,
   Start a rockin' 'round the clock again,
   We're gonna Rock Around The Clock tonight,
   We're gonna rock, rock, rock 'til broad daylight,
   We're gonna rock, gonna Rock Around The Clock tonight.

SAVE THE LAST DANCE FOR ME

Words and Music by
DOC POMUS and MORT SHUMAN

Moderately

You can dance ev - 'ry dance with the guy who
know that the mu - sic is fine, like

gave you the eye; let him hold you tight.
spark - ling wine; go and have your fun.

You can smile ev - 'ry
Laugh and sing but while

smile for the man who held your hand 'neath the
we're a - part don't give your heart to

pale moon - light. }
an - y - one. } But don't for -

get who's tak - ing you home and in whose arms you're

gon - na be. So

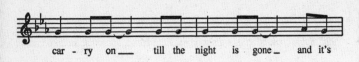

car - ry on __ till the night is gone __ and it's

time to go. __ If he asks if you're

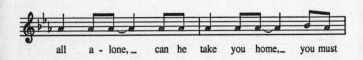

all a - lone, __ can he take you home, __ you must

tell him no. __ 'Cause don't for -

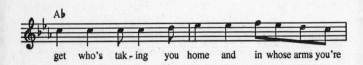

get who's tak - ing you home and in whose arms you're

gon - na be. __ So, dar - lin' __ Save The

Last Dance For Me. ____

RUNNING SCARED

**Words and Music by ROY ORBISON
and JOE MELSON**

Just Run-ning Scared, _____ feel-ing

low. _____ Run-ning Scared, _____

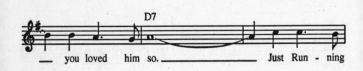

_____ you loved him so. _____ Just Run-ning

Scared, _____ a-fraid to lose. _____

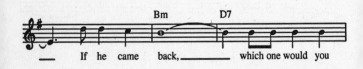

_____ If he came back, _____ which one would you

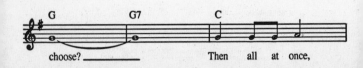

choose? _____ Then all at once,

he was stand-ing there, ___ *(Instrumental)* so

sure of him-self; ___ his head in the air. ___

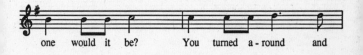

(Instrumental) My heart was break-ing; which

one would it be? You turned a-round and

walked a-way with me. *(Instrumental)*

Just Run-ning me. *(Instrumental)*

SEA OF LOVE

Words and Music by
GEORGE KHOURY and PHILIP BAPTISTE

SEE YOU LATER, ALLIGATOR

Words and Music by
ROBERT GUIDRY

Medium shuffle

Well, I saw my ba-by walk-ing, with an-oth-er man to-day.
told me, near-ly made me lose my head.

Well I saw my ba-by walk-ing, with an-oth-er man to-day.
When I thought of what she told me, near-ly made me lose my head.

When I asked her what's the mat-ter, this is what I heard her say:
But the next time that I saw her, remind-ed her of what she said.

See You Lat-er, Al-li-ga-tor, aft-er while, croc-o-dile;

See You Lat-er, Al-li-ga-tor, aft-er while, croc-o-dile.

Can't you see you're in my way, now. Don't you know you cramp my

1.
style? When I thought of what she

2.
style?

TAKE GOOD CARE OF MY BABY

Words and Music by
GERRY GOFFIN and CAROLE KING

SHAKE, RATTLE AND ROLL

Words and Music by
CHARLES CALHOUN

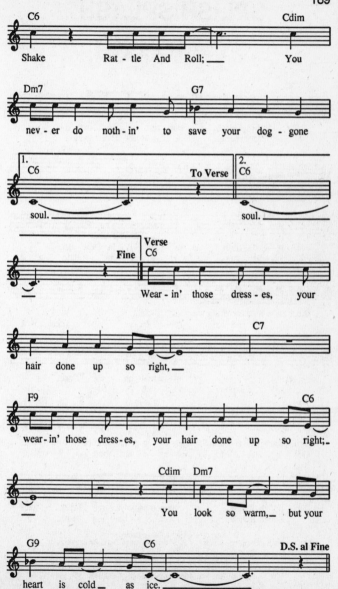

SPLISH SPLASH

Words and Music by
BOBBY DARIN and JEAN MURRAY

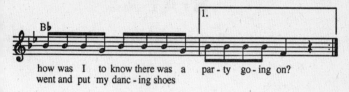

how was I to know there was a par - ty go - ing on?
went and put my danc - ing shoes

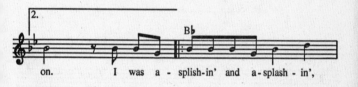

on.   I was a - splish-in' and a - splash - in',

I was a - roll - in' and a - stroll - in',

I was a - mov - in' and a - groov - in',

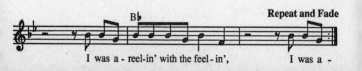

Repeat and Fade

I was a - reel-in' with the feel-in',   I was a -

STAY

Words and Music by
MAURICE WILLIAMS

Dance _____ just a lit - tle bit

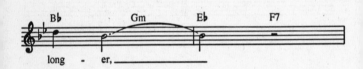

long - er, _____

please, please, please, please tell __ me that you're

go - in' to. _____ Now your

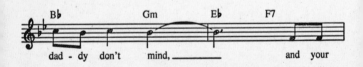

dad - dy don't mind, _____ and your

mom - my don't mind, _____ could we

have an - oth - er dance, dear?__ Just a - one more,

one _____ more _ time. Oh, won't you

Stay _____ just a lit - tle bit

long - er, _____ please let me

dance, _____ please say that you

will. _____

THE STROLL

Words and Music by
CLYDE OTIS and NANCY LEE

roll - ing. Stroll - ing__

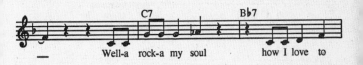

__ Well-a rock-a my soul how I love to

stroll._____ There's my love_____

__ stroll-ing in the door,__

there's my love_____ stroll-ing in the door.__

Ba - by, let's go stroll - ing

by the can - dy store._____

SUMMER IN THE CITY

Words and Music by JOHN SEBASTIAN,
STEVE BOONE and MARK SEBASTIAN

1.,3. Hot town, Sum-mer In The Ci-ty,
2.,4. Cool town, eve-nin' in the ci-ty,
(Instrumental last time)

Back o' my neck get-ting dir-ty and grit-ty.
Dressed up so fine and a look-in' so pret-ty.

Been down is-n't it a pi-ty;
Cool cat look-in' for a kit-ty;

Does-n't seem to be a shad-ow in the ci-ty.
Gon-na look in ev-'ry cor-ner of the ci-ty.

All a-round peo-ple look-in' half dead,
'Till I'm wheez-in' like a bus stop.

Walk-in' on the side-walk hot-ter than a match, yeah.
Run-nin' up the stairs gon-na meet you on the roof - top.___
(End instrumental) Yeah,___

But at night it's a dif-f'rent world;___

SURF CITY

Words and Music by
BRIAN WILSON and JAN BERRY

Bbm Gb

rear win - dow, __ but it still gets me where I
ev - 'ry guy __ and all you got - ta do is just
shoot-in'the curl __ and pick-in' out the par-ties for the

Eb Eb7

wan - na go. ___
wink your eye. ___
surf - er girl. ___

And I'm

Ab

goin' to Surf Cit - y 'cause it's two to one. You know I'm

goin' to Surf Cit - y, gon - na have some fun. Yea, I'm

Db

goin' to Surf Cit - y 'cause it's two to one. You know I'm

Ab

goin' to Surf Cit - y, gon - na have some fun. __

E F#7 1., 2. Eb

Two girls __ for ev - 'ry boy! ___

3. C

They say they two girls __ for
And if my

F G7 C

ev - 'ry boy! ___

SURFIN' U.S.A.

Music by CHUCK BERRY
Lyric by BRIAN WILSON

Solid Shuffle Beat

If ev-'ry-bod-y had an o - cean

route

a-cross the U. S. A. Then ev-'ry-bod-y'd be

we're gon-na take real soon. We're wax-in' down our

surf - in' like Cal-i-for-ni - a

surf - boards we can't wait for June.

You'd see them wear-in' their bag - gies,

We'll all be gone for the sum - mer,

huar-a-chi san-dals too.

we're on sa-fa-ri to stay.

A bush-y bush-y blonde hair-do,

Tell the teach-er we're surf - in',

Surf-in' U. S. A. You'll catch 'em surf-in' at

Surf-in' U. S. A. At Hag-gar-ty's and

Del Mar. Ven-tu-ra Coun-ty Line
Swam-i's, Pac-if-ic Pal-i-sades,

San-ta Cruz and Tress-els.
San O-no-fre and Sun-set,

Aus-tra-lia's Nar-a-bine.
Re-don-do Beach, L. A.

All o-ver Man-hat-tan
All o-ver La Jol-la,

and down Do-he-ny way. Ev-'ry-bod-y's gone
at Wai-a-me-a Bay. Ev-'ry-bod-y's gone

surf-in', Surf-in' U. S. A.
surf-in', Surf-in' U. S. A.

1.
We'll all be plan-nin' out a

2.

SWEET TALKIN' GUY

**Words and Music by DOUG MORRIS, ELLIOT GREENBERG,
BARBARA BAER and ROBERT SCHWARTZ**

In a steady four

Sweet Talk - in' Guy ____

talk - in' sweet kind of lies. ____

Don't you be - lieve in him. If you

do, he'll make you cry. He'll send you
(D.S.) Don't give him

flow - ers, then paint the town with an - oth - er girl. ____
love to - day. To - mor - row he's on his way. ____

He's a Sweet Talk - in' Guy, ____

but he's my kind of guy! ____

203

204

TALK THAT TALK

Words and Music by
SID WYCHE

With a beat

You ought to see my ba - by a -

walk-in' down the av - e - nue. Arm in arm with
yes, __ when she Talk That Talk. __ She's so dog-gone

me, __ it's a beau - ti - ful sight to
fine, __ when she tells me she's mine, all

see. __ You ought to hear my lov - in' ba -
mine. __ I want the world to see my ba -

- by whis - per in my ear __
- by, then they'll un - der - stand __ that

ten - der words __ she knows I love to hear. __
she's my love __ and I'm her lov - in' man. __

1.
B16   Eb E F N.C.   **To next strain**

You ought to see __ her

(LET ME BE YOUR)
TEDDY BEAR

Words and Music by
KAL MANN and BERNIE LOWE

THAT'LL BE THE DAY

Words and Music by
JERRY ALLSION, NORMAN PETTY and BUDDY HOLLY

With a beat

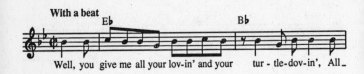

Well, you give me all your lov-in' and your tur-tle-dov-in', All

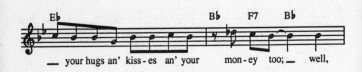

your hugs an' kiss-es an' your mon-ey too; well,

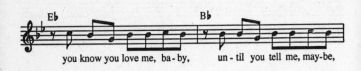

you know you love me, ba-by, un-til you tell me, may-be,

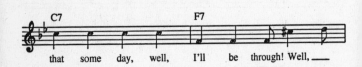

that some day, well, I'll be through! Well,

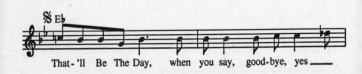

That-'ll Be The Day, when you say, good-bye, yes

That-'ll Be The Day, when you make me cry, ah, you

say you're gon - na leave, you know it's a lie,— 'cause

That-'ll Be The Day ————— when I die.— Well,

— when I die.— When Cu - pid shot his dart,

he shot it at your heart, so if we ev - er part and

I leave you, you say you told me an' you

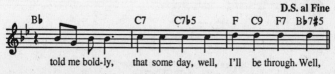

told me bold-ly, that some day, well, I'll be through. Well,

210

THAT'S ALL RIGHT MAMA

Words and Music by
ARTHUR CRUDUP

way   you _____   do. _____

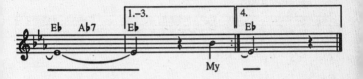

_____

My

_____

Additional Lyrics

3. I'm leavin' town tomorrow, leavin' town for sure,
   Then you won't be bothered with me hangin' 'round your door,
   But that's all right, that's all right.
   That's All Right, Mama, any way you do.

4. I oughta mind my papa, guess I'm not too smart.
   If I was I'd leave you, go before you break my heart,
   But that's all right, that's all right.
   That's All Right, Mama, any way you do.

THIS BOY
(RINGO'S THEME)

**Words and Music by JOHN LENNON
and PAUL McCARTNEY**

TIME WON'T LET ME

Words and Music by CHET KELLY
and TOM KING

TOBACCO ROAD

Words and Music by
JOHN D. LOUDERMILK

how I loathe___ this place called To-
proud to show___ give the name ___ To-

bac - co Road _____ but it's home.___
bac - co Road _____ but it's home.___

The on - ly

life I've - ev - er known { on - ly you
                              I de - spise.___

_____ know how I loathe.
_____ you 'cos you're filth - y. }

But I love___ you { To - bac - co
                     'cos you're home.___

1.
Road.

2.

Repeat and Fade

TUTTI FRUTTI

Words and Music by RICHARD PENNIMAN
and D. La BOSTRIE

I got a gal, her name's Sue, she knows just what to do.___ I've been to the east, I've been to the west, but she's the gal___ I love the best.___ Tut - ti Frut-ti au rut-ti, Tut - ti Frut-ti au rut-ti, Tut - ti Frut-ti au rut-ti, Tut - ti Frut-ti au rut-ti, Tut - ti Frut-ti au rut-ti, A - bop - bop - a - loom-op a -

I got a gal, her name's Dai - sy, she al - most drives me cra - zy. She's a real gone___ cook - ie yes - sir - ree, but pret - ty lit - tle Su - zy's the gal for me. ___

1.
lop bop boom! I got a

2.
lop bop boom!

TWIST AND SHOUT

**Words and Music by BERT RUSSELL
and PHIL MEDLEY**

UNDER THE BOARDWALK

Words and Music by ARTIE RESNICK
and KENNY YOUNG

Moderately, with a beat

Oh, when the sun beats down ___ and burns the
park you hear ___ the hap-py
(Instrumental)

tar up-on the roof. ___
sound of a car-ou-sel. ___

And your shoes get so hot you wish your
You can al-most taste the hot-

tired feet ___ were fire - proof.
dogs and french - fries they sell.
(End of Instrumental)

Un - der The Board - walk, ___

down by the sea, ___

P ON THE ROOF

Words and Music by
GERRY GOFFIN and CAROLE KING

WAKE UP LITTLE SUSIE

Words and Music by BOUDLEAUX BRYANT and FELICE BRYANT

Moderately bright

Wake Up, Lit-tle Su - sie, __ wake-up.

Wake Up, Lit-tle Su - sie, __ wake up.

We've both been sound a - sleep. __ Wake Up,
The mov - ie was-n't so hot. __ It did-

__ Lit-tle Su-sie, and weep. The mov - ie's o - ver, it's
n't have much of a plot. We fell a - sleep, __ our

four - o'clock __ and we're in trou - ble deep.
goose is cooked, __ our rep - u - ta-tion is shot. Wake Up, __ Lit - tle

Su - sie, __ Wake Up, __ Lit-tle Su - sie. __

Well, what are we gon - na tell your ma -

WHERE THE BOYS ARE

Words and Music by
HOWARD GREENFIELD and NEIL SEDAKA

Very slow

Bb   Gm   Dm

Where _____ The Boys Are

Cm7   F7   Bb

Some - one waits for me;   A

Cm7   F7   Bb   Gm

smil - ing face, a warm em - brace, two

Em7   A7   D   F7

arms to hold me ten - der - ly.

Bb   Gm   Dm

Where _____ The Boys Are

Cm7   F7   Bb

My true love will be.   He's

Cm7   F7   Bb   Gm

walk - ing down some street in town and I

WHO PUT THE BOMP
(IN THE BOMP BA BOMP BA BOMP)

Words and Music by
BARRY MANN and GERRY GOFFIN

Gm   Eb   F7

When my ba - by heard   bomp, ba - ba - bomp, ba - bomp -
Time that we're a - lone,   bomp, ba - ba - bomp, ba - bomp -

Bb

- ba - bomp - bomp,   ev - 'ry   word   went
- ba - bomp - bomp,   sets   my   ba - by's

Gm   Eb

right   in - to   her   heart._____
heart   all   a - glow._____

F7   Bb   Gm

___   And   when   she   heard   them   sing - ing
___   And   ev - 'ry   time   we   dance   to

Eb   F9#5   Eb7

ram - a - lam - a - lam - a - lam - a - ding - dong,
ram - a - lam - a - lam - a - lam - a - ding - dong,

Bb/F   Gm   Cm   F7   1. Bb

she   said   we'd   nev - er   have   to   part._____
she   al - ways   says   she   loves   me

2. Bb

___   so._____

WILD THING

Words and Music by
CHIP TAYLOR

I love you.
You move me.

Wild Thing, you make my heart sing.

You make ev - 'ry - thing __ groov - y, __

Wild Thing.

D.C. al Coda

CODA   Repeat and Fade

C'm'-on, _ c'm'-on, Wild Thing.

WILL YOU LOVE ME TOMORROW
(a/k/a WILL YOU STILL LOVE ME TOMORROW)

Words and Music by GERRY GOFFIN
and CAROLE KING

WOOLY BULLY

Moderately

1. Mat-ty told Hat-ty _____ A-bout a
2.,3. *(See additional lyrics)*

thing she saw. _____ Had

two big horns. _____ And a

wool - y jaw _____ Wool - y Bul - ly _____

_____ Wool - y Bul - ly _____

Wool - y Bul - ly _____ Wool - y

Bul - ly ___   Wool - y   Bul - ly ___

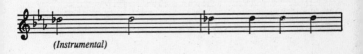

(Instrumental)

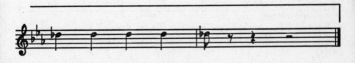

Additional Lyrics

2. Hatty told Matty
   Let's don't take no chance
   Let's not be L 7
   Come and learn to dance
   Wooly Bully-Wooly Bully-
   Wooly Bully-Wooly Bully-Wooly Bully.

3. Matty told Hatty
   That's the thing to do,
   Get yo' someone really
   To pull the wool with you–
   Wooly Bully-Wooly Bully-
   Wooly Bully-Wooly Bully-Wooly Bully.

WORKING IN THE
THE COAL MINE

Words and Music by
ALLEN TOUSSAINT

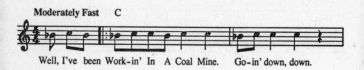

Well, I've been Work-in' In A Coal Mine. Go-in' down, down.

Work-in' In A Coal Mine. Whoo! A-bout to slip down.__

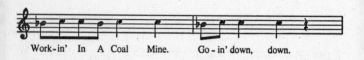

Work-in' In A Coal Mine. Go-in' down, down.

Work-in' In A Coal Mine. Whoo! A bout to slip down.__

__ Five o'clock in the morn - in',

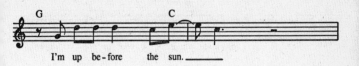

I'm up be-fore the sun. ____

When my work-day is o - ver, I'm

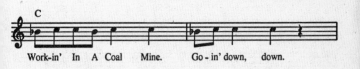

too tired for hav-in' fun. ____ I've been

Work-in' In A Coal Mine. Go-in' down, down.

Work-in' In A Coal Mine. Whoo! A-bout to slip down. ____

Work-in' In A Coal Mine. Go-in' down, down.

240

Work-in' In A Coal Mine. Whoo! A - bout to slip down.

(Instrumental)

(Spoken:) Lord! I am so tired!

How long can this go

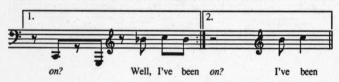

1.
on? Well, I've been

2.
on? I've been

C
work - in', go - in'

Repeat and Fade

work - in'. Whoo! A - bout to slip down.

YOUNG BLOOD

Words and Music by
JERRY LEIBER, MIKE STOLLER & DOC POMUS

1. Eb Bb7#5 Eb
2. Eb Eb7

Ab

What cra-zy stuff   she looked so tough

Eb   Cm7

I had to fol-low her   all the way home. ___

F7

Then things went bad,   I met her dad, he said,

Bb7 N.C.   Bb9

Spoken: "You bet-ter leave   my   daugh-ter a-lone!" ___ Well,

Eb

I could-n't sleep a wink for try - ing, _____

I saw the ris-ing of the sun,

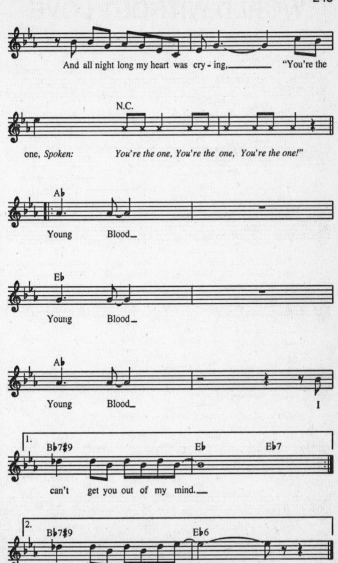

WORLD WITHOUT LOVE

Words and Music by
JOHN LENNON and PAUL McCARTNEY

Please lock me a - way __ And don't al - low the
Birds sing out of tune __ And rain - drops hide the

day _____ here in - side _____ Where I
moon. ____ I'm O. K. ____ Here I'll

hide ____ with my lone - li - ness. _____
stay ____ with my lone - li - ness. _____

_____ I don't care what they say I won't

stay ____ in A World With - out Love.

Love.   So I wait and

in a while __ I will see my true love smile. __

Abm   Fm7

She may come I know not when. When she does I'll

Cb   Bb7   Eb

know, So ba - by un - til then lock me a - way

G7   Cm

And don't al - low the day here in -

Eb   Ab6

side Where I hide with my

Eb

lone - li - ness. I don't

Fm7   Bb7

care what they say I won't stay in A World With - out

Eb   C7   Fm7

Love. I don't care what they say I won't

Bb7   Eb

stay in A World With - out Love.

YOU REALLY GOT ME

Words and Music by
RAY DAVIES

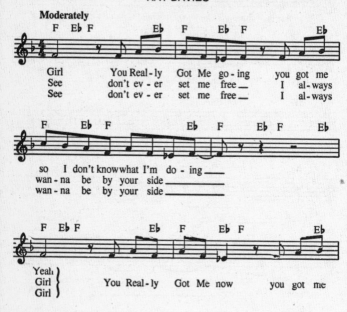

Girl   You Real-ly Got Me go-ing   you got me
See   don't ev-er set me free___   I al-ways
See   don't ev-er set me free___   I al-ways

so I don't know what I'm do-ing___
wan-na be by your side_____
wan-na be by your side_____

Yeah
Girl }   You Real-ly   Got Me now   you got me
Girl

so   I can't sleep at night

Yeah   You Real-ly Got Me now   you got me

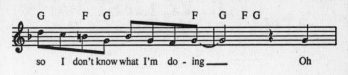

so I don't know what I'm do-ing___ Oh

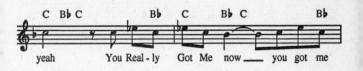

yeah You Real-ly Got Me now___ you got me

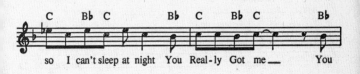

so I can't sleep at night You Real-ly Got me___ You

Real-ly Got Me___ You Real-ly Got Me___

1. *(Instrumental)* 2. Oh oh___

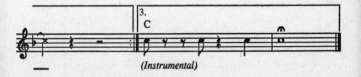

___ 3. *(Instrumental)*

YOU'VE LOST
THAT LOVIN' FEELIN'

Words and Music by BARRY MANN,
CYNTHIA WEIL and PHIL SPECTOR

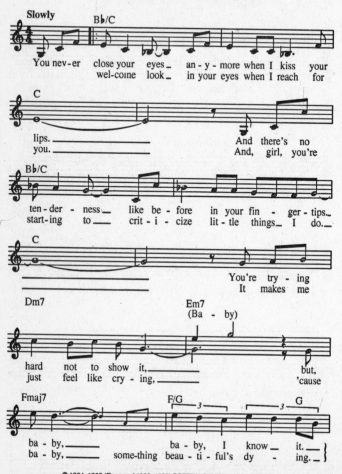

You nev-er close your eyes _ an-y-more when I kiss your
wel-come look _ in your eyes when I reach for

lips. _ And there's no
you. _ And, girl, you're

ten-der-ness _ like be-fore in your fin - ger-tips.
start-ing to _ crit-i-cize lit-tle things _ I do.

_ You're try - ing
It makes me

hard not to show it, _ but,
just feel like cry-ing, _ 'cause

ba - by, _ ba-by, I know _ it. _
ba - by, _ some-thing beau-ti-ful's dy - ing. _

You've Lost ___ That Lov - in' Feel - in',

woh oh, that lov - in' feel - in'.

You've Lost That Lov - in' Feel - in'! Now it's

gone, gone, gone, woh oh oh oh. ___

Now there's no

Ba - by, ba - by, I'd get down on my knees for

you. ___ If you would on - ly

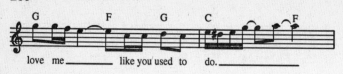

love me _____ like you used to do. _____

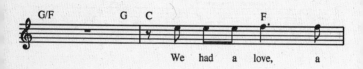

We had a love, a

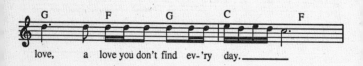

love, a love you don't find ev-'ry day. _____

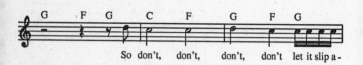

So don't, don't, don't, don't let it slip a-

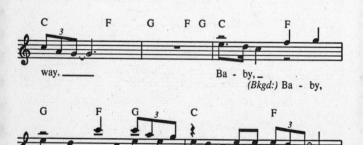

way. _____ Ba - by, _
(Bkgd:) Ba - by,

ba - by, I beg you please, _____
ba - by, _____ beg you please, _____

GUITAR CHORD FRAMES

	C	Cm	C+	C6	Cm6
C		3 fr			

	C#	C#m	C#+	C#6	C#m6
C#/Db		4 fr		3 fr	2 fr

	D	Dm	D+	D6	Dm6
D					

	Eb	Ebm	Eb+	Eb6	Ebm6
Eb/D#	3 fr				

	E	Em	E+	E6	Em6
E					

	F	Fm	F+	F6	Fm6
F					

This guitar chord reference includes 120 commonly used
chords. For a more complete guide to guitar chords, see
"THE PAPERBACK CHORD BOOK" (HL00702009).

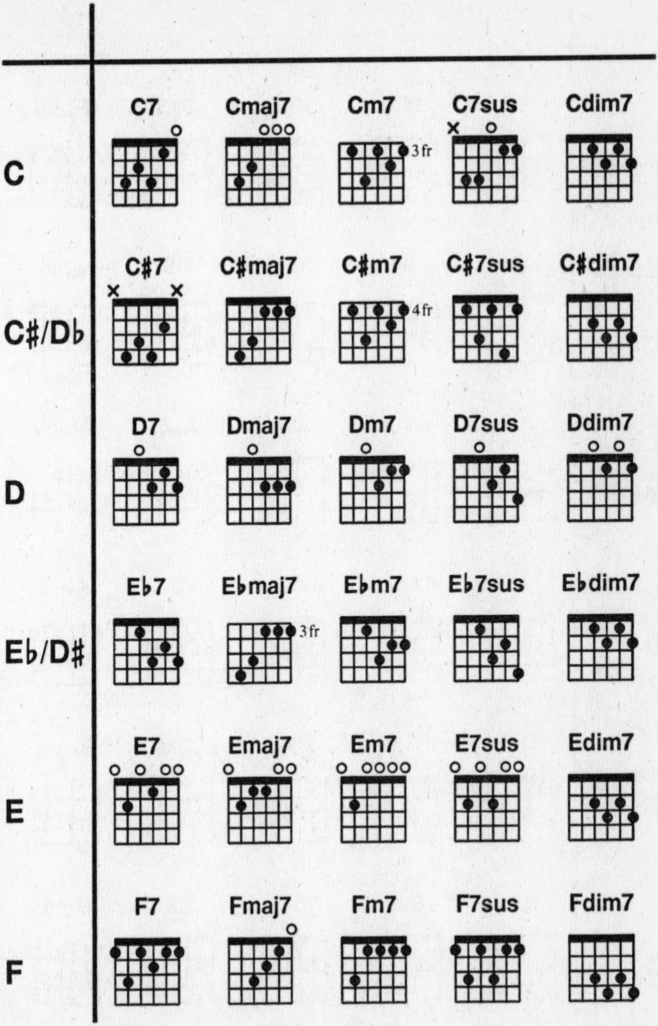
C
C7
Cmaj7
Cm7
3 fr
C7sus
Cdim7
C♯/D♭
C♯7
C♯maj7
C♯m7
4 fr
C♯7sus
C♯dim7
D
D7
Dmaj7
Dm7
D7sus
Ddim7
E♭/D♯
E♭7
E♭maj7
3 fr
E♭m7
E♭7sus
E♭dim7
E
E7
Emaj7
Em7
E7sus
Edim7
F
F7
Fmaj7
Fm7
F7sus
Fdim7

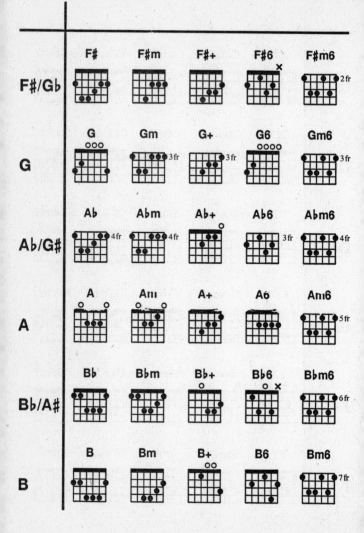

F#/Gb	F#7	F#maj7	F#m7	F#7sus	F#dim7
G	G7	Gmaj7	Gm7	G7sus	Gdim7
Ab/G#	Ab7	Abmaj7	Abm7	Ab7sus	Abdim7
A	A7	Amaj7	Am7	A7sus	Adim7
Bb/A#	Bb7	Bbmaj7	Bbm7	Bb7sus	Bbdim7
B	B7	Bmaj7	Bm7	B7sus	Bdim7

These perfectly portable paperbacks include the melodies, lyrics, and chords symbols for your favorite songs, all in a convenient, pocket-sized book. Using concise, one-line music notation, anyone from hobbyists to professionals can strum on the guitar, play melodies on the piano, or sing the lyrics to great songs. Books also include a helpful guitar chord chart. A fantastic deal - only $5.95 each!

THE BEATLES
00702008 ....$5.95

THE BLUES
00702014 ....$5.95

CHORDS FOR KEYBOARD & GUITAR
00702009 ....$5.95

CLASSIC ROCK
00310058 ....$5.95

COUNTRY HITS
00702013 ....$5.95

THE ROCK & ROLL COLLECTION
00702020 ....$5.95

FOR MORE INFORMATION, SEE YOUR LOCAL MUSIC DEALER,
OR WRITE TO:

HAL•LEONARD™
CORPORATION

7777 W. BLUEMOUND RD. P.O. BOX 13819 MILWAUKEE, WI 53213